A Gathered Garden

 3-Dimensional Fabric Flowers

15 Projects — Quilts & More

Mix and Match Bouquets

Carol Armstrong

C&T PUBLISHING INC.

Text © 2004, Carol Armstrong
Artwork © 2004 C&T Publishing

PUBLISHER: Amy Marson
EDITORIAL DIRECTOR: Gailen Runge
EDITOR: Pamela Mostek
TECHNICAL EDITORS: Carolyn Aune, Joyce Engels Lytle
COPYEDITOR: Linda Dease Smith
PROOFREADER: Eva Simoni Erb
COVER DESIGNER: Christina Jarumay
BOOK DESIGNER: Kathleen Tandy
DESIGN DIRECTOR: Diane Pedersen
ILLUSTRATOR: Matt Allen
PRODUCTION ASSISTANT: Tim Manibusan
QUILT PHOTOS: Kirstie McCormick
HOW-TO PHOTOS: Diane Pedersen
Published by C&T Publishing, Inc., P.O. Box 1456,
   Lafayette, California, 94549

FRONT COVER: *Flower Basket*
BACK COVER: *Gathered Circle Garden, Watering Can, Basket*

Attention Copy Shops: Please note the following exception—Publisher and author give permission to photocopy pages 22, 25, 26, 29, 30, 33, 36, 37, 38, 41, 42, 43, 44, 47, 48, 51, 52, 55, 56 and 59 for personal use only.

Attention Teachers: C&T Publishing, Inc. encourages you to use this book as a text for teaching. Contact us at 800-284-1114 or www.ctpub.com for more information about the C&T Teachers Program.

We take great care to ensure that the information included in this book is accurate and presented in good faith, but no warranty is provided nor results guaranteed. Having no control over the choices of materials or procedures used, neither the author nor C&T Publishing, Inc. shall have any liability to any person or entity with respect to any loss or damage caused directly or indirectly by the information contained in this book. For your convenience, we post an up-to-date listing of corrections on our website (www.ctpub.com). If a correction is not already noted, please contact our customer service department at ctinfo@ctpub.com or at P.O. Box 1456, Lafayette, California, 94549.

Trademarked (™) and Registered Trademark (®) names are used throughout this book. Rather than use the symbols with every occurrence of a trademark and registered trademark name, we are using the names only in the editorial fashion and to the benefit of the owner, with no intention of infringement.

LIBRARY OF CONGRESS CATALOGING-IN-PUBLICATION DATA

Armstrong, Carol.
  A gathered garden : 3-dimensional fabric flowers, 15 projects, quilts & more, mix & match bouquets / Carol Armstrong.
    p. cm.
  Includes index.
  ISBN 1-57120-262-5 (paper trade)
  1. Appliqué--Patterns. 2. Quilts. 3. Fabric flowers. I. Title.
TT779.A7585 2004
746.44'5--dc22
                                    2003027741

Printed in China
10 9 8 7 6 5 4 3 2 1

Table of Contents

Introduction

The gathered circle or yo-yo has been a friend of mine since I was a child. When I was ten years old, a visit to a girlfriend's house was my first introduction to this country art form. Her grandmother had sewn a yo-yo coverlet to adorn every bed and every chair in their home! The bright colors and texture of the design charmed me instantly.

Years later, I discovered an unfinished piece of these gathered circles living quietly in a trunk. I began it with my youthful excitement and made it from my mother's sewing scraps. Running across this much-loved piece inspired me to try playing with those gathered circles once again.

What fun! My love of appliqué, quilting, and flowers combined to create gathered floral creations with added dimension using my new yo-yos. But I didn't stop there. The gathered flowers I created just called out to be popped onto wire stems. They became flowers that any fabric lover will adore. Even a fabric bead with a wonderful textural quality evolved from the gathered circles. Using these fun yo-yo creations, now you can even have jewelry from your favorite quilt fabric!

Whether you quilt or make craft or bead projects, you're sure to find a project that's just perfect for you. I encourage you to experiment with new designs using these gathered circle creations. Flowers and fabric are always an inspiration for me, and I hope they are the same for you. Enjoy the book.

Tools and Materials

 efore you get started making your own yo-yo creations, you'll need to gather a few supplies. Many of them you'll have on hand and others you may have to locate or purchase. I recommend getting them all together before you begin. That way you won't have to stop and look for things when you'd rather be putting together your fabric flowers.

Here's What You'll Need:

Basic sewing supplies—good sharp scissors, needles, pins, and a thimble are a good start.

Cutting mat, acrylic ruler, and rotary cutter—great for squaring up quilts and accurately cutting border and binding strips

Fabrics—for appliqué background fabric I use preshrunk, wrinkle-resistant, unbleached muslin. This is also good for backing. For appliqué and yo-yos, lightweight 100% cotton fabrics are best. If you use a fabric that is too heavy, it will not gather easily into a nice circle. Color? Just have fun with all the colors and prints that you like. A print will change in tone after it has been gathered into a circle. Add to your stash and play!

Sewing thread—regular sewing thread in colors to match the appliqué and yo-yo fabrics. For quilting use a thread specifically designed for quilting. You may like a heavy thread such as carpet or button weight for adding flowers to quilts. I usually use a double strand of all purpose thread for this.

Batting—for inside the quilts I prefer Poly-Fil Traditional. It gives nice dimension to the quilting. For lining some of the appliqué shapes, a light-weight cotton batting works well.

Stuffing—for filling some of the fruit, you'll need polyester stuffing or shredded batting.

Fusible web—this can be used for one version of leaf construction. Use your favorite fusible web and follow the manufacturer's directions.

Cardstock or template plastic—to make templates for cutting fabric circles and leaves

Beads—for flower centers or jewelry, use sizes 4mm to 10mm, depending on your preference and project. The bead needs to be bigger than the hole in the yo-yo. They can be wood, plastic, or glass.

Buttons—small buttons may be substituted for the bead flower centers. They also make great embellishments.

Stem wire—for the stemmed flowers I use 26 gauge white cloth-covered stem wire. Any floral wire will work as long as it will go through the bead. You can change the color of the cloth-covered stem wire with markers, paint, or dye.

Floral tape—a waxed-paper tape for wrapping stems. It comes in green and white.

Beading cord—for stringing necklaces

Pre-made leaves (optional)—available in the floral or wedding department

Craft glue—a thick white glue works well for securing flower and leaf components.

Round toothpicks—to spread glue and help in creating fabric beads

Marking tools—I use a blue removable marker on light fabrics. A white fabric marker works well for darker fabrics. Don't iron any marks as they may set permanently. For straight quilt lines, masking tape works well. For short-term marking, press the tip of the needle into the fabric and "draw" a line.

Lightbox—excellent for tracing appliqué and quilting designs onto fabric. A glass table with a light underneath or a window on a sunny day will also work.

Small needle-nose pliers—to bend and cut wire

Awl—for creating holes in the fabric yo-yos. A round toothpick or a large blunt needle will also work.

Turning stick—for turning leaves. I use a blunt-end sharpened dowel, but a chopstick or slightly blunted wooden skewer works well also.

Basic Appliqué

The quilts in this book all use very basic hand appliqué. In this section you will find easy step-by-step instructions for the hand-appliqué technique as well as information on how to secure the yo-yo flowers and other creations to your quilt.

To begin, place the pattern on a lightbox. Position the background fabric, right side up, over the pattern and secure with a few pins if you like. Using a removable marker, trace the entire design onto the background. Remove the background but not the pattern from the lightbox.

Select the fabric for each appliqué piece. With the pattern on the lightbox, trace each individual appliqué piece onto the right side of the fabric using a removable marker.

Cut out each piece leaving about a ³⁄₁₆" turn-under allowance.

Stitch each piece onto the background using the pre-marked design on the background fabric as a guide. If the order of appliqué is important, the pieces are numbered on the pattern. Pieces that are covered by another are appliquéd first. I use a tack stitch for appliqué.

Appliqué Stitch

As you stitch each piece, use the needle to turn under the allowance to the line on the appliqué piece, matching it with the motif lines on the background. Turn under and sew only those edges that are exposed, not those that will be covered by another piece.

Some of the projects in the book include appliquéing batting-lined pieces to the quilt, such as *Still Life Fruit Bowl* on page 49. Stitch on the seamline of the lined pieces to keep a nice smooth edge on the piece. The openings that were left for turning the piece right side out will be sewn closed as you appliqué.

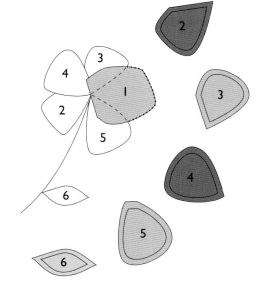

Inside Curves

Clip the turn-under allowance almost up to the turn-under line on pieces that have inside curves such as the basket handle on page 45.

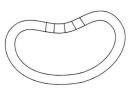

Points

Most of the leaves have points that are simple to sew. Square off the end of the point, leaving a ³⁄₁₆" turn-under allowance. Fold under the seam allowance straight across the point. Bring your thread up through the exact point, hiding the knot in the fold. Take one stitch into the background.

Hold down the end of the appliqué. Using the shaft of the needle, turn under a portion of the allowance beyond the point and stitch. Continue stitching to the next point.

Make a stitch at the exact point on your appliqué shape. Take a tiny second stitch to secure the piece. Clip the excess fabric at the point.

Push under the allowance using your needle and stitch. Continue stitching to finish the piece. Remember these are leaf points and nature is not always perfect. Relax. Allow little differences to be part of the piece.

 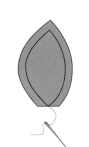 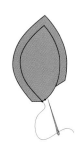  

| Square off the end of point. | Bring thread through at exact point. | Take one stitch into background. | Continue stitching to point. | Make stitch at the exact point. |

Bias Stems

For narrow bias lines, such as flower stems, I cut the strip about ½" wide so it is easy to handle. Finger-press one side and stitch in place along the marked line on the background.

Flip the piece open to expose the turn-under allowance. Carefully trim the allowance close to the stitching, leaving enough fabric to secure the piece. Flip the piece back. Trim to double the width needed for the stem.

Needle-turn the allowance as you stitch down the other side. You will be surprised how easy it is to create nice narrow stems. Some fabrics will cooperate better than others. The lighter weight ones are friendlier for this technique. If a fabric doesn't cooperate, making it difficult to get a cleanly turned edge, pick a different one.

Finger press and stitch in place.

Flip open and trim.

Flip back and trim.

Turn in allowance and stitch.

Stem Stitch

There are several projects with embroidered stems. As the name says, use the stem stitch for them. I use two strands of floss and a single line of stitching for tiny stems and two or more parallel lines for thicker stems.

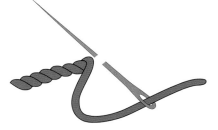

Making the Garden

Making the flowers, leaves, and other components is fun and easy to do. Here you'll find step-by-step instructions to construct them. When you create the projects in the book, refer back to this section for details on how to put the individual flowers together. Make your project uniquely your own by experimenting with different fabrics and colors, or make changes in the flowers you use.

. . . .

Basic Yo-Yo

The flowers are all constructed of several size yo-yos, which is a gathered circle of fabric. So that you'll be prepared to make all the flowers in the book, make templates from template plastic or cardstock by tracing around each of the circles shown on page 59.

To make it easier to keep track of your yo-yo templates, write the size of the circle on each with a permanent marking pen. Keep them all together in a plastic bag.

1. Cut out a fabric circle that is the size indicated for each flower. Turn under a small hem around the circle and run a gathering thread, using one or two strands of matching thread.

2. Pull the thread tight to form the circle. Secure with three or four small stitches in the folds. Run the thread inside the circle and out again. Snip thread.

Use a medium-length stitch when gathering the yo-yos. A stitch that is too tiny will not give you very good gathers. Try a few practice yo-yos until you're happy with the results. Use a smaller hem for the small gathered circles. Try some practice ones and find the hem and gathering stitch that bring you the best results.

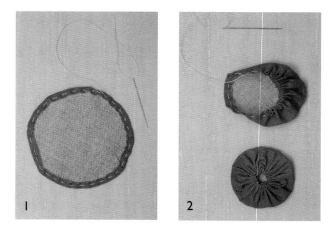

Stem and Center

This unit is used for all the stemmed flowers. Cut a stem twice the desired length and slide on a bead. Pull the wire around the bead.

If you have trouble getting a wire through a bead, try cutting the wire at an angle. Or just try a different bead as the hole sizes often vary.

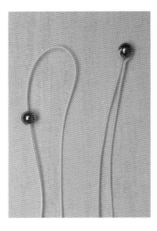

The Fabric Bead

1. Make three yo-yos of the same size. Place two back-to-back and whipstitch the edges together halfway around, using a matching thread. Open the unstitched halves of the two connected yo-yos and insert the third yo-yo to form a three-sided bead.

2. Whipstitch the edge of the third yo-yo to the edge of one of the connected yo-yos. To keep a hole open, slide a round toothpick into the center and stitch the last edges together.

Leaves

One option is to use pre-made leaves from floral or wedding departments of craft and fabric stores. They are great for craft projects and add a nice textural change from the fabrics of the flowers. If you prefer, you can make your own leaves following these steps.

Fused Leaves

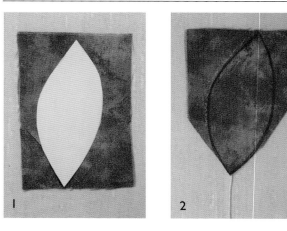

1. Iron paper-backed fusible web to the wrong side of a piece of fabric that is slightly larger than the leaf. Using one of the patterns on page 59, draw a leaf on the right side of the fabric. Remove the paper backing. Cut a stem the desired length plus 1" and place on the fusible side of the fabric. Position another piece of fabric on top with wrong sides together.

2. Trim the edge of the leaf on the drawn line at the stem end. Fuse following the manufacturer's instructions.

3. Cut the leaf shape and wrap the stem with floral tape.

Sewn Leaves

1. Cut two leaves from fabric using one of the patterns on page 59. With right sides together, stitch around the leaf, leaving the space between the dots open.

Cut a length of stem wire the desired length plus 1" or 2". Bend one end of the wire down slightly less than the length of the leaf. Turn the cut end up to prevent it from coming through the leaf. Turn the leaf right side out, using a small turning stick. Press.

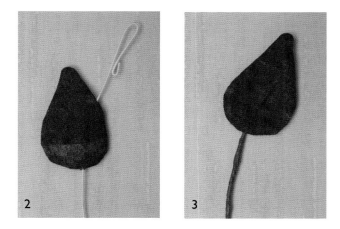

2. Use an awl to pierce a hole in the bottom of the leaf. Slide the unfolded end of the wire into the unstitched opening and then through the hole at the bottom of the leaf. Glue the folded end of the stem before pulling it into the leaf.

3. Carefully pull the wire into the leaf and press it to the leaf fabric. Glue the leaf opening closed. Wrap the stem with floral tape.

The Flowers

Before we begin the instructions for the individual flowers, here are a few things to keep in mind:

- The sizes stated in the patterns are the size of the cut circle, not the size of the finished yo-yo.

- The top of the yo-yo is the gathered side.

- Each flower begins with a beaded stem, see page 11.

- Use the awl with a twisting and piercing motion to make the holes through the yo-yo centers without breaking too many threads.

- From the stem bottom, slide the flower components upward on the stem in top-to-bottom order.

- You can add a little glue between yo-yos if you like. Try a few flowers and decide your preference.

- Starting just below the stem, wrap the floral tape around the stem several times to get it started. Then wrap several more times, spiraling downward. Push this beginning wrap upward on the stem to secure the flower components tightly up against the bead center. Continue wrapping, adding leaves or other flowers as you choose. Stretching the floral tape slightly as you wrap helps the wax surface stick to itself.

To cut several circles for your flowers, it is easy to use a rotary cutter, ruler, and cutting mat. Cut the squares the same size as the diameter of the circle, then stack them up with the circle template on top and cut off the corners.

Floret

Make:
• Two 1¾" yo-yos

1. Add glue between the yo-yos. The floret is made singly but may be wrapped with others to form a multi-blossom flower.

Saucer Flower

Make:
• One 1½" yo-yo
• One 4" yo-yo
• One 1¾" yo-yo for the base

1. Run a gathering thread just inside the edge of the 4" yo-yo. Draw the thread up slightly to form a shallow cup. Secure the gathering thread with a few tiny stitches on the back.

Poppy

Make:
• One 1½" yo-yo
• One 4" yo-yo
• One 1¾" yo-yo for the base

1. For this variation of the saucer flower, run the gathering thread ¼"–⅜" from the edge of the 4" yo-yo. Draw this thread up to form a hat shape when the flower is upside down.

Five-Petal Posie

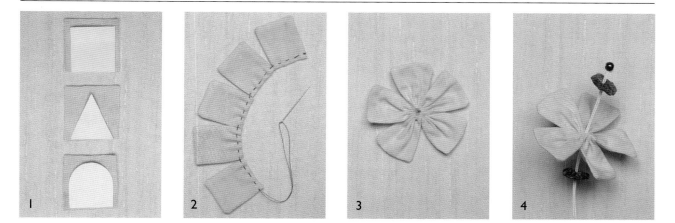

Make:
• One 1½" yo-yo
• One 1½" yo-yo for the base

1. You will need five petals for each posie, which can be made in different shapes. For each flower, start with ten 1½" x 1½" squares. Using the patterns on page 59, draw one of the petal shapes onto five of the squares.

2. With right sides together stitch each pair along the drawn line, leaving the bottom open. Trim ⅛" beyond the stitched line, turn, and press. Line up the five petals and run a gathering thread through them ⅛" from the raw edges.

3. Draw up the thread to gather the petals into a circle. Secure the thread.

4. Sew or glue the top and base yo-yos in place. Add the stem and wrap. If you sew, appliqué the top and base yo-yos to the petals before inserting the stem. If you use glue, add it as you slide the pieces on the stem.

Bead Rose

Make:
- Three 2" yo-yos
- One 1½" yo-yo for the base

1. Follow the instructions for a fabric bead on page 11. Slide the stem through the hole formed by the toothpick. Push the fabric bead and base tightly up to the center bead, flattening the fabric bead and wrapping the stem with floral tape. This flower works well in groups and can be made from any size bead.

Bead Center Posie

Make:
- Three 1½" yo-yos
- One 3" yo-yo
- One 1½" yo-yo for the base

1. Follow the instructions for the fabric bead on page 11. Assemble and push the fabric bead up tightly to flatten slightly as you wrap.

Berry

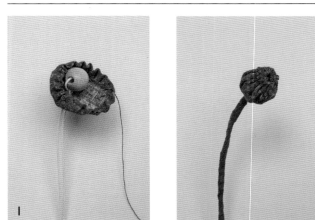

Make:
- One 1¾" yo-yo (Before gathering, pierce a hole in center.)

1. Attach a 10 mm bead to the stem, referring to page 11. Slide the stem through and gather the yo-yo up over the bead. Secure the thread with several small stitches in the gathers. Increase the size of the bead and yo-yo for larger berries.

Stuffed Bead Fruit

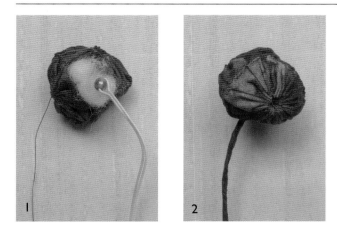

Make:
• Three yo-yos (any size)

1. Follow Step 1 of the fabric bead instructions on page 11. When you are ready to stitch the last edges, omit using the toothpick. Add a small amount of stuffing and insert the bead of the beaded stem inside the fruit.

2. Stitch the fruit completely closed, catching the stem bead inside to attach the stem.

Rose

Make:
• Two 1½" yo-yos
• Two 2" yo-yos
• Four 2½" yo-yos (two pairs)
• One 1½" yo-yo for the base

1. This flower is composed of four sets of two yo-yos stitched together, with a 6mm or 8mm bead on the stem.

Using a tiny whipstitch, stitch the pairs with top sides together. For the 1½" pair, stitch just short of ½ way around; for the 2" pair, stitch ¼ way around; for the 2½" pairs, stitch ⅛ way around.

2. With the tops of the yo-yo units up, slide the stem through the centers of the seams. Alternate the directions of the petals. Use the awl to make the holes for the stems, avoiding breaking the whipstitch threads. Wrap the stem.

Bud

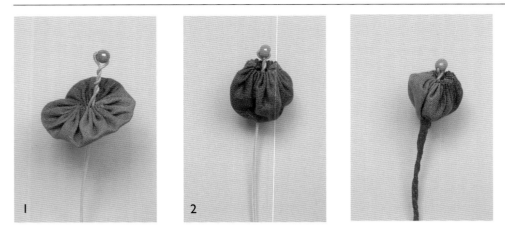

Make:
• One 2½"–4" yo-yo for the bud

1. Twist the beaded stem for about ¼" down from the bead.

2. Slide the yo-yo onto the stem. Pull the bottom down to make a teardrop shape. Allow the bead to extend beyond the yo-yo. Hold the bottom tightly to the stem and start wrapping, catching some of the yo-yo fabric in the wrap. Don't push the wrap up as with other flowers.

Four-Petal Tulip

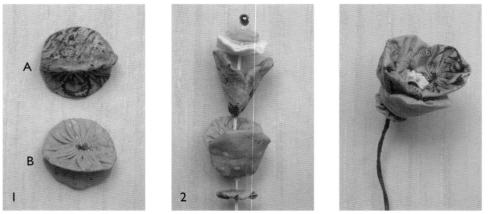

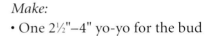

Make:
• One 1½" yo-yo
• One 2½" yo-yo
• Four 3" yo-yos (two pairs)
• One 1¾" yo-yo for the base

1. For the inside pair (A) whipstitch two 3" yo-yos with top sides together just short of ½ the distance around. For the outside pair (B), whipstitch two 3" yo-yos with bottom sides together just short of ½ the distance around. After sewing, turn to put top sides inside.

2. Slide pair A, the inside pair, into pair B, the outside pair, with the petals opposite. Place all parts on the stem.

Make:
- One 1¾" yo-yo
- One 2" yo-yo
- Three 3" yo-yos
- One 2" yo-yo for the base

1. With bottom sides together, whipstitch two 3" yo-yos ¼ the distance around the edge. Insert the third yo-yo and stitch on either side ¼ the distance around. This will make a cup shape.

2. Turn so the top sides of the yo-yos are inside the cup. Assemble.

Adding Flowers to the Quilt

After you've completed your flowers, it's time to add them to your quilt. For stemless flowers, make all of the components listed for the flower except the base yo-yo. Then sew the flowers directly to the quilt after the quilting is done. Stitch through all three layers of the quilt to secure.

After knotting a double thread, take two stitches in place through all layers where the flower is attached on the top of the quilt. Slide the flower components on the thread from the bottom up. Thread the bead and go back through all the components to the back of the quilt and secure the thread.

When you're sewing a flower onto your quilt, you may find that a small bead wants to go through the hole in the yo-yo. To prevent this, allow the stitches to go through the gathers on either side of the hole.

Now you're ready to enter the gathered garden with this delightful assortment of ideas for quilts and other fun projects. Refer to the instructions in the Making the Garden section to make each of the components for your gathered creation. The instructions for each project tell you just what you need to cut, then use the photo and patterns as guides for positioning the flowers, leaves, and other details.

Elegant Roses

Finished size: 14" x 18"

The soft ivory and muted green fabrics give this simple quilt an elegant feel.
An iridescent glass bead at each rose center finishes the picture
with just a touch of glitz.

Materials and Cutting

Fabric requirements are based on approximately 42"-wide cotton fabric.

For the appliqué shapes, use the Elegant Rose pattern on page 22. Refer to Basic Appliqué on page 7 for information on marking and cutting the pieces.

Fabric	Cutting
½ yard muslin for background and backing	One 10½" x 14½" piece for background; one 16" x 20" piece for backing
⅛ yard first medium green for inner border	Two 1½"-wide strips
¼ yard dark green for outer border	Two 2¼"-wide strips
Small pieces assorted medium and dark greens for leaves and stems	17 leaves; three ½"-wide bias strips approximately 9" long for stems
Small pieces light, medium, and dark cream for roses	From patterns on page 59, six 2" light cream circles; twelve 2½" medium cream circles; six 1½" dark cream circles
¼ yard second medium green for binding	Two 2"-wide strips
Batting	16" x 20"

Other Materials:
• 3 beads (8mm)
• threads to match appliqué and yo-yo fabrics
• natural-color quilting thread

Assembly

1. Refer to Basic Appliqué on page 7 to stitch the flowers, leaves, and stems to the background. Appliqué the stems onto the background in the order shown. Appliqué leaves 4, 5, and 6, then add the rest of the leaves in any order.

2. Remove any markings and press. Trim the background to 8½" x 12½".

3. Add the medium green inner border and dark green outer border to the quilt, referring to page 60.

4. Baste for quilting, referring to page 60. Quilt random triangles at the bottom of the stems and wavy lines upward. Quilt-in-the-ditch around the background and the inner border. Remove any markings and basting.

5. Add the binding to the quilt, referring to page 61.

6. Make three roses from the cream fabrics, referring to page 17. Omit the base yo-yo. Using the beads, attach the roses to the stem ends, referring to page 19.

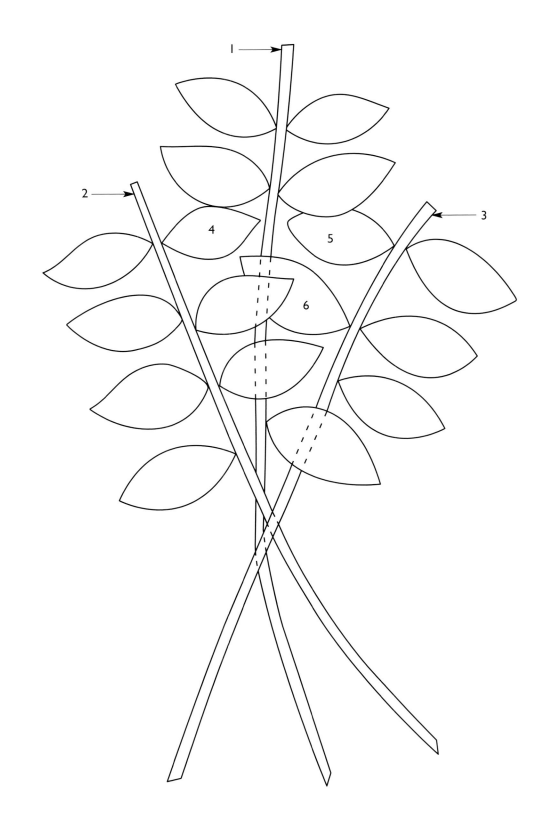

Elegant Roses Pattern

Gathered Circle Garden

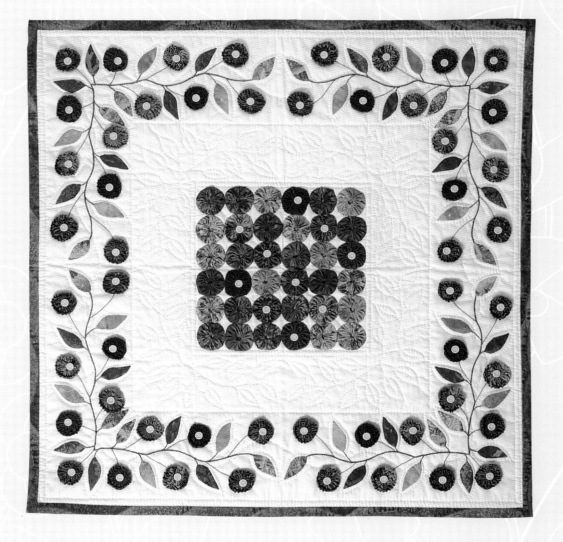

Finished size: 26½" x 26½"

Pick your favorite colors to fill this yo-yo garden.
Small buttons make quick and easy flower centers.
The leafy appliqué and quilting design
add to the formal feel.

Materials and Cutting

Fabric requirements are based on approximately 42"-wide cotton fabric.

For the appliqué leaves, use the Gathered Circle Garden patterns on pages 25–26. Refer to Basic Appliqué on page 7 for information on marking and cutting the pieces.

Materials	Cutting
1¾ yards muslin for background and backing	One 28" x 28" square for the background; one 28" x 28" square for the backing
Small pieces assorted greens for leaves and center yo-yos	56 leaves; from pattern on page 59, twenty-six 3" circles
Small pieces assorted purples for saucer flowers and center yo-yos	From pattern on page 59, sixty-two 3" circles (52 for the saucer flowers and 10 for center yo-yos)*
⅓ yard green for binding	Four 2"-wide strips
Batting	28" x 28"

Other Materials:
- 1 skein of embroidery floss in each of 2 different greens
- 62 small buttons
- threads to match appliqué and yo-yo fabrics
- natural-color quilting thread

Note: This is different from the 4" size mentioned in the individual flower directions.

Assembly

1. Connect the sections of the pattern on pages 25–26, and make a full-size pattern for appliqué and embroidery placement. Sew a small stitch in contrasting thread onto the background to mark the dots noted on the pattern. These are reference points that can be ironed. Mark the appliqué and embroidery lines on the background with a removable marker. (You will mark the quilting lines later.)

2. Refer to Basic Appliqué on page 7 to stitch the leaves to the quilt. Appliqué the leaves to the background.

3. Using two strands of floss, embroider the stems, referring to page 9. Stitch two lines of stem stitch for the main stem and one line for the side stems. Remove any markings and press.

4. Using the thread dots to realign the background on the pattern, mark the quilting lines with a removable marker. Baste for quilting, referring to page 60. Quilt and remove markings and basting.

5. Trim the edge ½" from the last line of quilting and add binding, referring to page 61.

6. Make the flat center yo-yos and appliqué them to the center square, randomly placing the colors. You may have to adjust their positions to fit evenly.

7. Make 52 purple saucer flowers, referring to page 14. Omit the base yo-yos and center yo-yos. Using a button for each flower center, attach the saucer flowers to the stem ends, referring to page 19. Add buttons to some of the yo-yos in the center block.

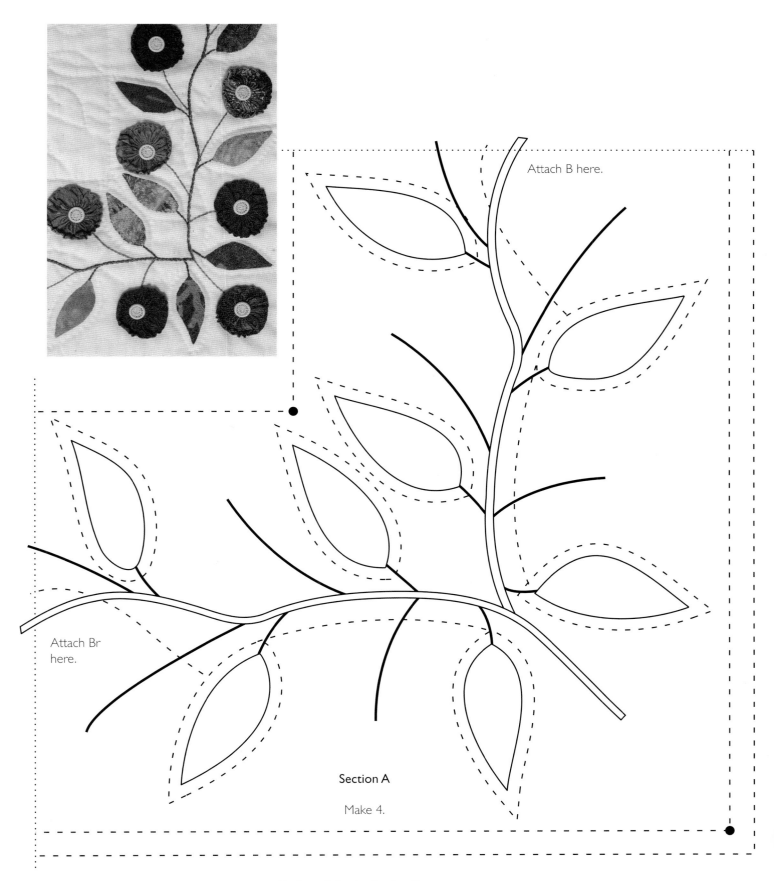

Attach B here.

Attach Br
here.

Section A

Make 4.

Gathered Circle Garden Pattern

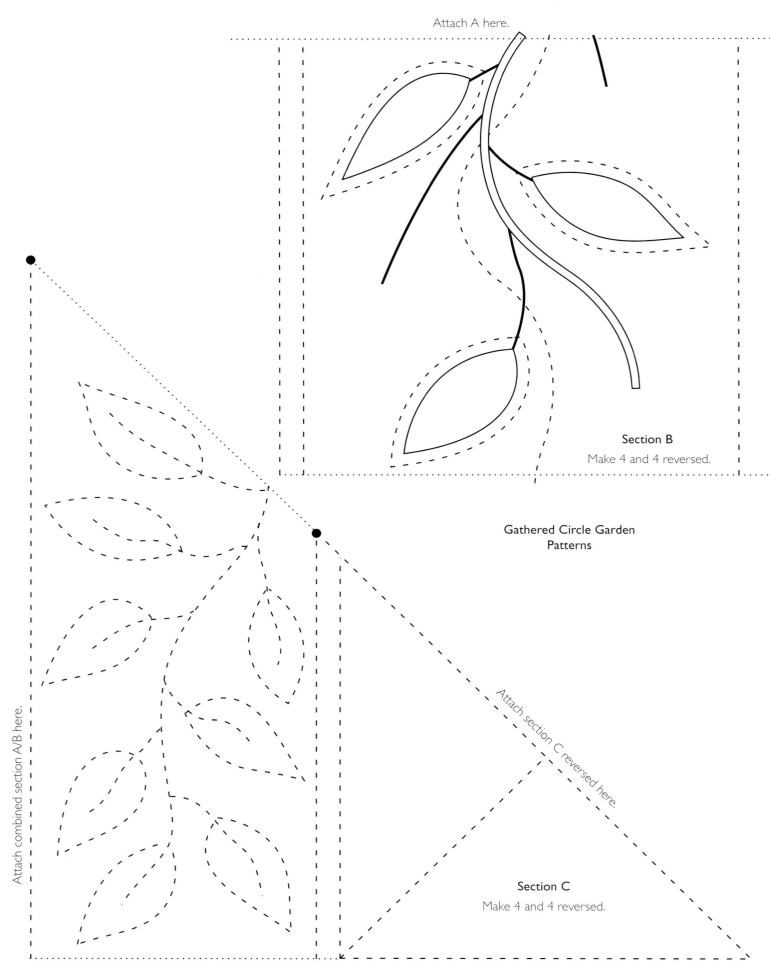

Attach A here.

Section B
Make 4 and 4 reversed.

Gathered Circle Garden
Patterns

Attach section C reversed here.

Attach combined section A/B here.

Section C
Make 4 and 4 reversed.

Garden Wreath

Finished size: 19½" x 19½"

Wreath blocks are always a wonderful way to show off flower designs. Here is an idea to get you started. Mix and match your favorite blooms and colors.

Materials and Cutting

Fabric requirements are based on approximately 42"-wide cotton fabric.

For the appliqué shapes, use the Garden Wreath patterns on pages 29–30. Refer to Basic Appliqué on page 7 for information on marking and cutting the pieces.

Fabric	Cutting
⅔ yard muslin for background and backing	One 14" x 14" square for background; one 21" x 21" square for backing
⅓ yard print for border	Two 4"-wide strips
Small pieces assorted blues, yellows, and reds for flowers	From patterns on page 59, seven 1½" yellow circles; eleven 1¾" yellow circles; nine 2" red circles; seven 4" blue circles for flowers
Small pieces assorted greens for leaves and stems	33 leaves; two ½"-wide bias strips approximately 18" long for stems
¼ yard green for binding	Two 2"-wide strips
Batting	21" x 21"

Other Materials:
- 11 red, 7 blue, and 3 pearl beads (4mm or 6mm)
- 1 skein of green embroidery floss
- threads to match appliqué and yo-yo fabrics
- natural-color quilting thread

Assembly

1. Refer to Basic Appliqué on page 7 to stitch the leaves and stems to the quilt. Appliqué the main stems to the background using the bias strip. Add the assorted leaves.

2. Using two strands of floss, embroider the smaller stems with two rows of stem stitch, referring to page 9.

3. Remove any markings and press. Trim the background to 12½" x 12½".

4. Add the print border to the quilt, referring to page 60.

5. Baste for quilting, referring to page 60. Quilt sections of radiating lines, each section running a different direction. Masking tape makes stitching straight lines simple. Remove any markings and basting.

6. Add binding to the quilt, referring to page 61.

7. Make seven blue saucer flowers, referring to page 14. Do not gather the edges and omit the base yo-yos. Make three red bead roses, referring to page 16. Omit the base yo-yo. Make eleven yellow yo-yos.

8. Attach the flowers to the stem ends, referring to page 19 and matching the colored dots with the flowers. Use the blue beads for the saucer flowers, pearls for the bead roses, and the red beads for the simple yo-yos.

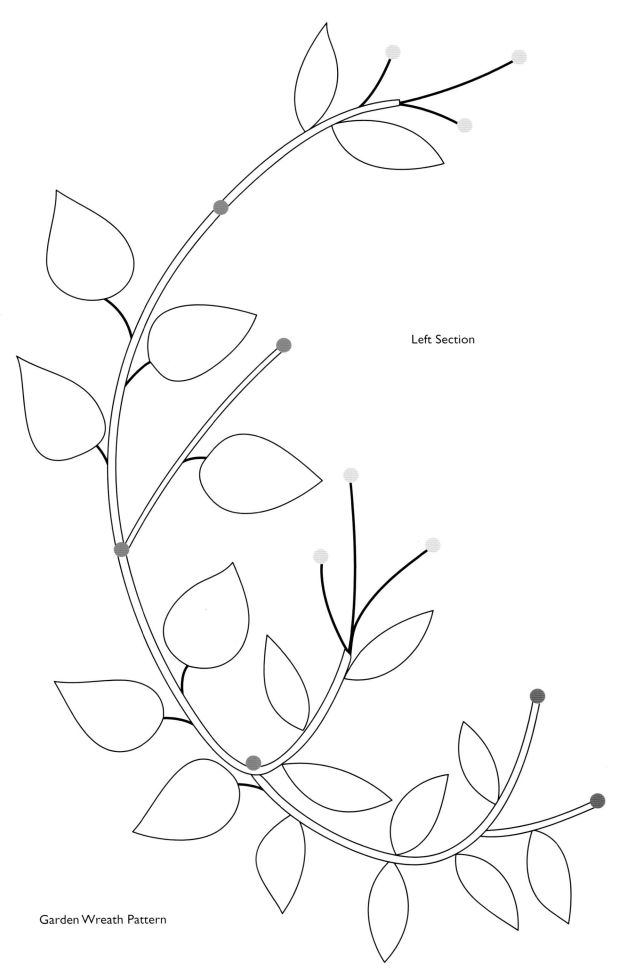

Left Section

Garden Wreath Pattern

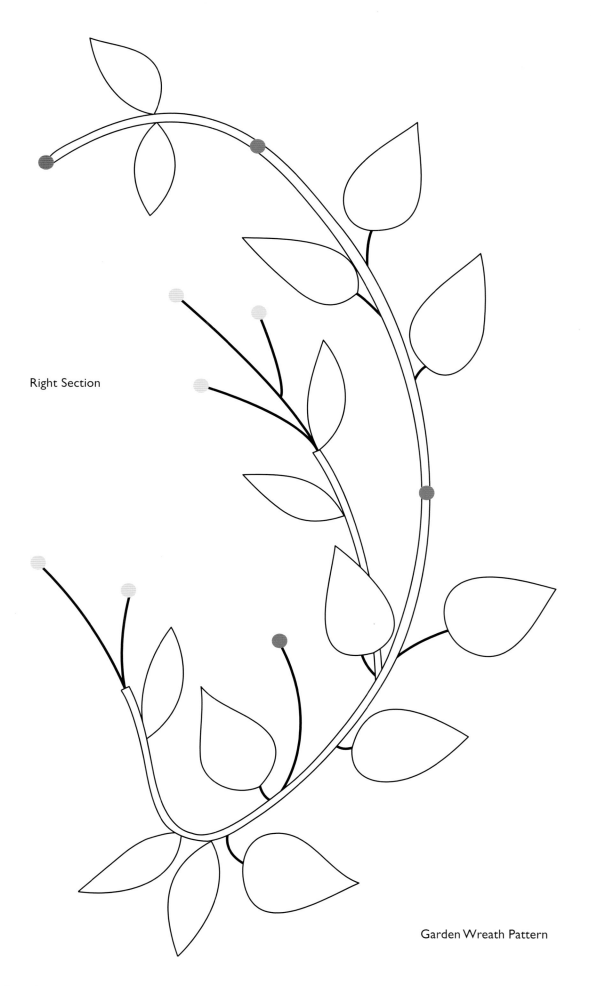

Right Section

Garden Wreath Pattern

Sweet and Simple

Finished size: 15½" x 29½"

*P*retty in pink! Or yellow or blue
or any favorite flower color.
Let a floral print border inspire your
sweet and simple quilt.

Materials and Cutting

Fabric requirements are based on approximately 42"-wide cotton fabric.

For the appliqué shapes, use the Sweet and Simple pattern on page 33. Refer to Basic Appliqué on page 7 for information on marking and cutting the pieces.

Fabric	Cutting
1 yard muslin for background and backing	Three 8½" x 9½" pieces for background; one 18" x 32" piece for backing
⅓ yard **dark green** for sashing and inner border	Two 2" x 7½" pieces for sashing; two 2"-wide strips for inner border
⅜ yard **pink print** for outer border and corner squares	Three 3"-wide strips for outer border; four 2" x 2" squares for corner squares
⅛ yard **pink** for flowers	From pattern on page 59, thirty-six 2" pink circles
Small pieces assorted greens for leaves	21 leaves
¼ yard **medium green** for binding	Three 2"-wide strips
Batting	18" x 32"

Other Materials:
• 12 green beads (4-6mm.)
• 1 skein green embroidery floss
• threads to match appliqué and yo-yo fabrics
• natural-color quilting thread

Assembly

1. Refer to Basic Appliqué on page 7 to stitch the leaves to the quilt. Appliqué the assorted green leaves onto the three muslin blocks. Using two strands of floss, embroider the stems with two rows of stem stitch, referring to page 9.

2. Remove any markings and press. Trim the blocks to 6½" x 7½".

3. Sew the two dark green sashing pieces between the three muslin blocks.

4. Add the dark green side border to the quilt, referring to page 60. Sew the pink print corner squares to the top and bottom border and sew to the quilt.

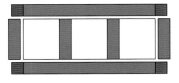

5. Add the pink print border to the quilt, referring to page 60.

6. Baste for quilting, referring to page 60. Quilt as shown, using ¾"-wide masking tape to easily mark the straight lines. Remove any markings and basting.

7. Add binding to the quilt, referring to page 61.

8. Make 12 bead roses from the 36 pink circles, referring to page 16. Omit the base yo-yos. Using the green beads, attach the roses to the stem ends, referring to page 19.

Sweet and Simple Pattern

Make 3.

𝓜ake it even more simple by creating
one sweet bouquet, rather than three.
Make it for a charming accent for your home
or a thoughtful gift for a special friend.
Very Sweet and Simple!

Buttercup Blocks

Finished size: 29½" x 29½"

The five-petal flowers make this simple pieced design come alive.
This is a great project for those floral fabrics in your stash.

Materials and Cutting

Fabric requirements are based on approximately 42"-wide cotton fabric.

For the appliqué shapes, use the Buttercup Blocks patterns on pages 36–38. Refer to Basic Appliqué on page 7 for information on marking and cutting the pieces.

Fabrics	Cutting
1½ **yards muslin** for blocks and backing	One 12" x 12" square for center block; four 16" x 8" pieces for appliquéd border panels; one 32" x 32" square for backing
⅓ **yard first green** print for triangle blocks and stems	Two 8" x 8" squares (cut each once diagonally for triangle blocks); ½"-wide bias strips approximately 135" long (total) for stems
¼ **yard second green** print for corner blocks	Four 5½" x 5½" squares
½ **yard third green** print for border	Four 3"-wide strips
⅓ **yard yellow** for flower petals	From the pattern on page 59, one hundred seventy 1½" x 1½" yellow squares
⅛ **yard white** for flower centers	From the pattern on page 59, seventeen 1½" circles
⅜ **yard fourth green** for leaves and binding	40 leaves; four 2"-wide strips
Batting	32" x 32"

Other Materials:
• 17 dark beads (6mm-8mm)
• threads to match appliqué and yo-yo fabrics
• natural-color quilting thread

Assembly

1. Refer to Basic Appliqué on page 7 to stitch the leaves and stems to the quilt. Connect the sections of the pattern on pages 36–37 and make full-size patterns for appliqué placement. Appliqué the stems onto the center square and border panels in the order shown, referring to page 7. Add the leaves.

2. Remove any markings and press. Trim the center square to 10½" x 10½" and the border panels to 5½" x 14¾".

3. Sew two green triangles to opposite sides of the appliquéd center square using a ¼" seam allowance. Press outward. Repeat to sew the triangles to the remaining sides.

4. Sew two appliquéd border panels to the sides of the quilt. Sew the corner squares to the ends of the two remaining border panels. Sew to the top and bottom.

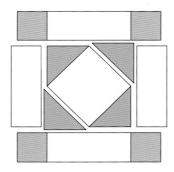

5. Add outside border to the quilt, referring to page 60.

6. Baste for quilting, referring to page 60. Quilt using masking tape to mark the straight lines. Quilt around the blocks and the appliqué. Remove any markings and basting.

7. Add binding to the quilt, referring to page 61.

8. Make 17 five-petal flowers using the rounded edge petal, referring to page 15. Omit the base yo-yos. Using the dark beads, attach the five-petal flowers to the stem ends, referring to page 19.

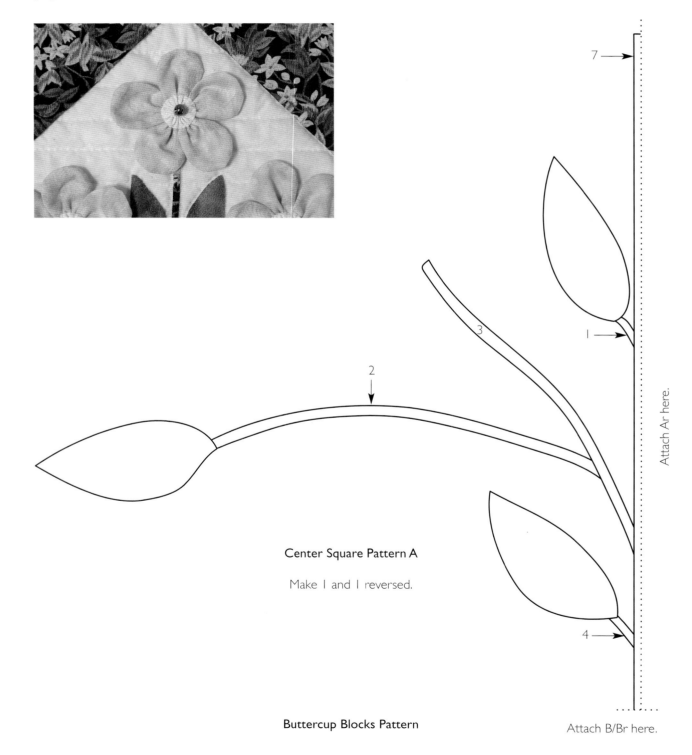

Center Square Pattern A

Make I and I reversed.

Buttercup Blocks Pattern

7 →

3

2

1 →

Attach Ar here.

4 →

Attach B/Br here.

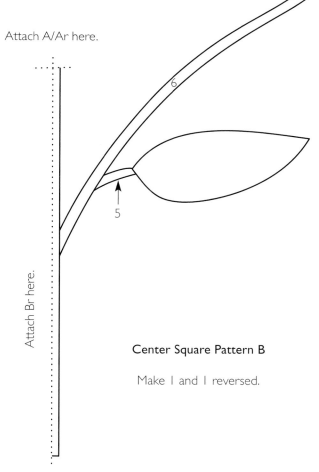

Attach A/Ar here.

6

5

Attach Br here.

Center Square Pattern B

Make 1 and 1 reversed.

Buttercup Blocks Pattern

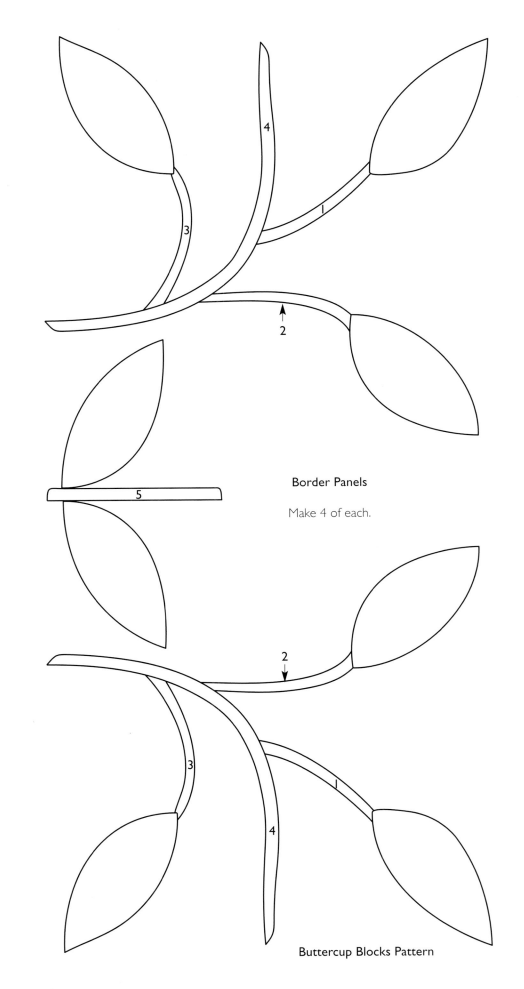

Border Panels

Make 4 of each.

Buttercup Blocks Pattern

Flowers All in a Row

Finished size: 15½" x 25½"

Let your garden grow!
This row of leafed stems can be topped
with many combinations of gathered flowers.
This version combines hot reds and oranges
with a touch of cool blue.

Materials and Cutting

Fabric requirements are based on approximately 42"-wide cotton fabric.

For the appliqué shapes, use the Flowers All in a Row patterns on pages 41–44. Refer to Basic Appliqué on page 7 for information on marking and cutting the pieces.

Fabric	Cutting
1 yard muslin for background and backing	One 12" x 22" piece for background; one 18" x 28" piece for backing
¼ yard print for border	Two 3"-wide strips
Small pieces orange for flowers	From the patterns on page 59, two 3" circles for bead center posies; five 1¾" circles for florets; four 2" circles for roses
Small pieces red for flowers	Five 1¾" circles for florets; eight 2½" circles for roses
Small pieces gold for flowers	Six 1½" circles for bead center posies; one 1½" circle for saucer flower; four 1½" circles for roses; ten 1½" squares for five-petal flower
Small pieces blue for flowers	One 4" circle for saucer flower; one 1½" circle for five-petal flower; three 1¾" circles for berries
Small pieces assorted greens for leaves	Assorted leaves
¼ yard red for binding	Three 2"-wide strips
Batting	18" x 28"

Other Materials:
- 11 assorted beads for flower centers
- 3 beads for inside berries (10mm)
- 1 skein green embroidery floss
- threads to match appliqué and yo-yo fabrics
- natural-color quilting thread

Assembly

1. Using two strands of floss, embroider all the stems, except for the berry plant, referring to page 9. Use two rows of stem stitch for the main stems and one row for short stems.

2. Refer to Basic Appliqué on page 7 to stitch the leaves to the quilt. Using the same appliqué stitch, join the parts of the five-petal posie leaves together before you appliqué them to the background. Do not stitch into the turn-under allowance around the outside of the leaf. If left free, the seam allowance will turn under more easily when you appliqué it to the background. Clip curves as needed.

3. Appliqué the leaves to the quilt. Embroider the berry stem over the leaves.

4. Remove any markings and press. Trim the background to 10½" x 20½".

5. Add the border, referring to page 60.

6. Baste for quilting, referring to page 60. Quilt groups of arched parallel lines in the sky in the background and border. Quilt clamshells in the spaces created. Add some simple leaf shapes through the center area. Echo with lines about ¼" apart. Remove any markings and basting.

7. Add binding to the quilt, referring to page 61.

8. Make 2 bead center posies, referring to page 16; 1 saucer flower, referring to page 14; 5 florets, referring to page 14; 1 five-petal posie with pointed petals, referring to page 15; 3 berries, referring to page 16; and 2 roses, referring to page 17. Omit the base yo-yos on all flowers. The berries use 10mm plastic beads with a yo-yo drawn up over them. Stitch the berries to the quilt by catching the bottom fabric to the background with a few stitches. Attach the flowers, referring to page 19.

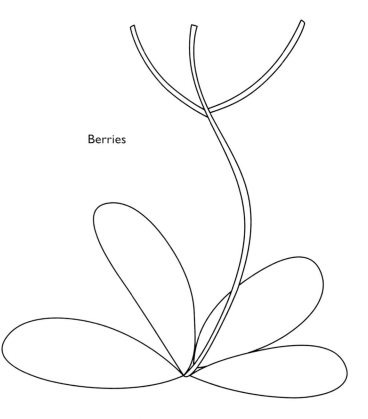

Berries

Flowers All in a Row Pattern

Bead Center Posie

Saucer Flower

Flowers All in a Row Patterns

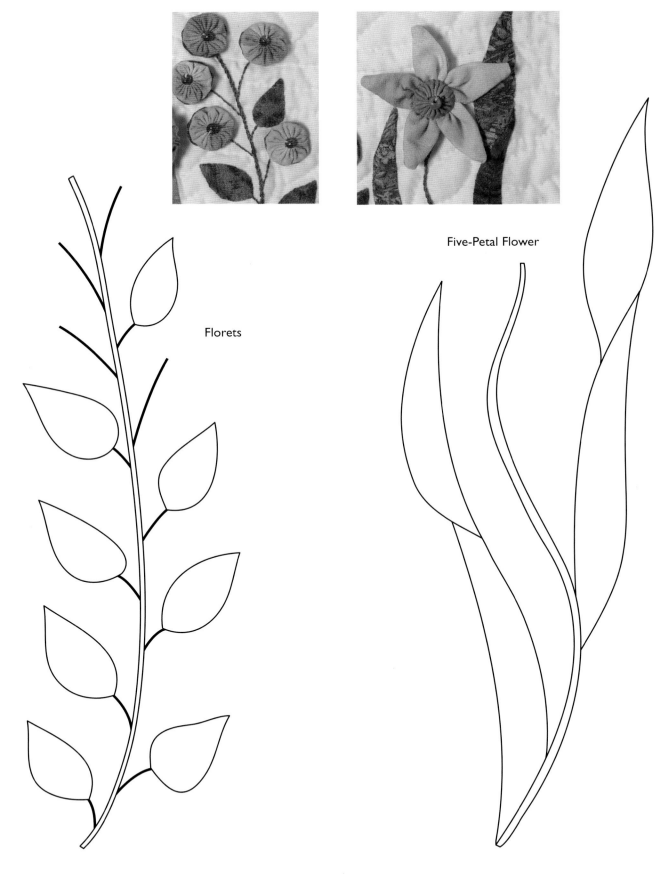

Five-Petal Flower

Florets

Flowers All in a Row Patterns

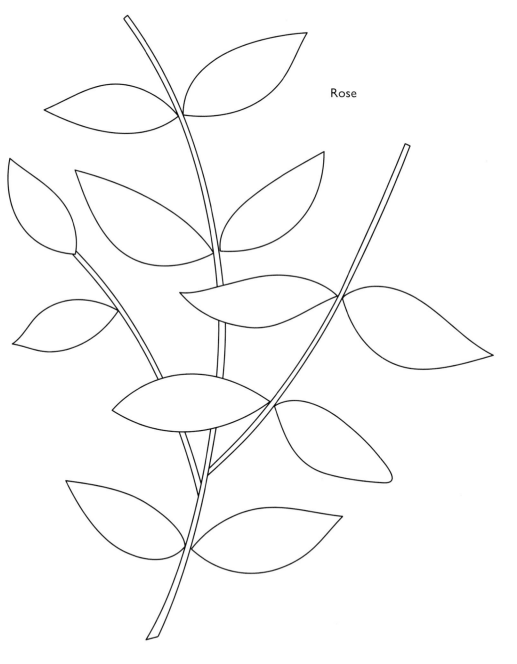

Rose

Flowers All in a Row Pattern

Flower Basket

Finished size: 20½" x 20½"

*T*his project combines traditional quilt design
with the delightful stemmed gathered flowers.
What fun! Keep the quilt colors basic and you can change the flowers
to suit the season. They easily slide out of the quilted basket.

Materials and Cutting

Fabric requirements are based on approximately 42"-wide cotton fabric.

For the appliqué shapes, use the Flower Basket patterns on pages 47–48. Refer to Basic Appliqué on page 7 for information on marking and cutting the pieces.

Fabric	Cutting
¾ yard muslin for background and backing	One 14½" x 14½" square for the background; one 22" x 22" square for backing
⅓ yard green print for border	Two 3½"-wide strips
¼ yard dark green for binding	Three 2"-wide strips
¼ yard gold print for handle and basket	One of handle pattern on page 47 and two of basket pattern on page 48.
Small pieces assorted greens, blues, yellows, oranges, pinks, and reds for stemmed flowers and leaves	Choose from the flowers on pages 14–19 and use the patterns needed for each.
Cotton batting for basket	12" x 6"
Batting for quilt	22" x 22"

Other Materials:
• Wire, beads, floral tape, glue (optional)
• threads to match appliqué and yo-yo fabrics
• natural-color quilting thread

Assembly

1. From the pattern on page 47, trace around half of the handle, then flip and trace to make the complete handle. Cut out and trace the pattern onto the gold fabric, adding ¼" turn-under allowance to the edge.

2. Refer to Basic Appliqué on page 7 to stitch the handle to the background fabric.

3. Remove any markings and press. Add the border, referring to page 60.

4. Baste for quilting, referring to page 60. Trace the leaf quilting pattern on page 47. Quilt the background area with the leaf template in a random and overlapping pattern. Quilt behind the basket area to keep the quilt flat. Quilt two lines approximately ¼" apart along the inner edge of the border. Add random clamshells outward by echoing to the outer edge of the border. Remove any markings and basting.

5. Add binding to the quilt, referring to page 61.

6. Position the two gold basket pieces with right sides together on top of the 12" x 6" piece of cotton batting.

7. Sew around the outside edge of the basket and batting, using a ¼" seam. Leave a 2" opening at the bottom. Trim the excess batting close to the seamline and clip seam allowances as needed. Turn right side out and press. It isn't necessary to sew the opening closed. Quilt with a few simple vertical lines about 1" apart.

8. Appliqué the quilted basket onto the background. It's all right if the stitches go through to the back, but it's not necessary. Stitch around, except for the three openings shown on the top of the pattern. Use a few extra stitches at all the dots to secure.

9. To fill my basket I used three five-petal posies on page 15, one saucer flower on page 14, one three-petal tulip on page 19, and leaves on page 12. To make a basket of flowers uniquely your own, fill it with flowers and berries of your choice. Slide the stems into the slots at the top of the basket.

Leaf pattern for background quilting

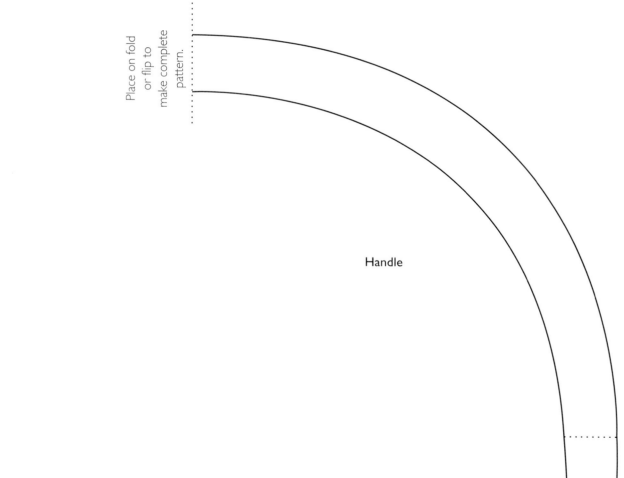

Place on fold or flip to make complete pattern.

Handle

Flower Basket Patterns

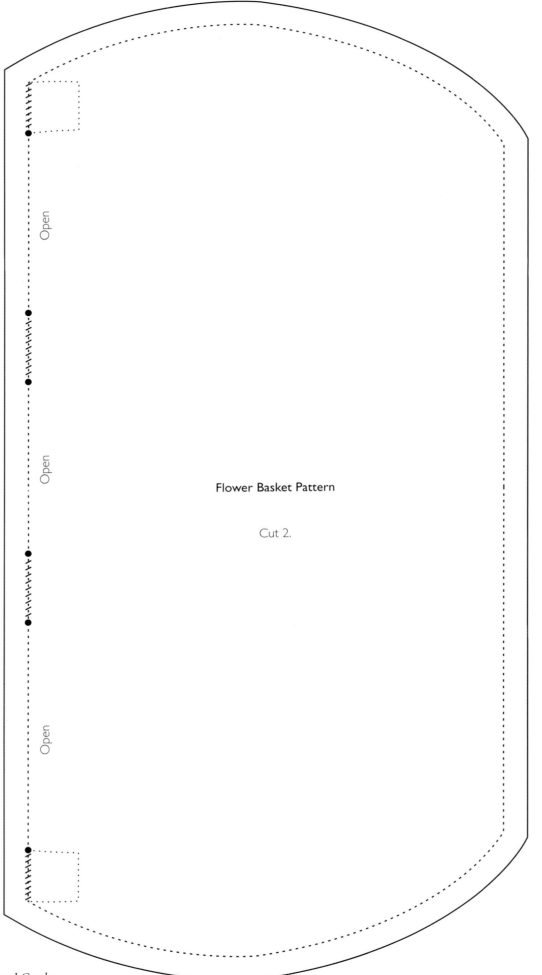

Open

Open

Flower Basket Pattern

Cut 2.

Open

Still Life Fruit Bowl

Finished size: 17½" x 19½"

Fill your bowl with nature's delicious bounty.
In this delightful quilt the background fruits are lightly stuffed and appliquéd.
The stemmed berries and cherries look freshly picked
as they slip easily into the bowl.

Materials and Cutting

Fabric requirements are based on approximately 42"-wide cotton fabric.

For the appliqué shapes, use the Still Life Fruit Bowl patterns on pages 51–52. Refer to Basic Appliqué on page 7 for information on marking and cutting the pieces.

Fabric	Cutting
⅔ yard muslin for background and backing	One 12½" x 14½" for background; one 20" x 22" for backing
¼ yard print for border	Two 3"-wide strips
¼ yard red for binding	Three 2"-wide strips
¼ yard brown for bowl	One of Patterns A and C, two of Pattern B on page 51
Small pieces assorted greens for appliquéd leaves	4 leaves
Small pieces assorted yellows, greens, blues, and reds for stemmed fruit and leaves	From the patterns on page 59, seven 1¼" blue circles for blueberries, twelve 2" red circles for cherries, and eight green leaves
Cotton batting for bowl and fruit lining	12" x 6"
Batting	20" x 22"

Other Materials:
- wire, floral tape, glue (optional)
- 11 beads (10mm)
- 1 skein green embroidery floss
- threads to match appliqué and yo-yo fabrics
- natural-color quilting thread

Assembly

1. Refer to Basic Appliqué on page 7 to stitch the leaves and bowl pieces A and C to the background. Appliqué the four leaves onto the background, using the photo and bowl pattern for placement. Using two strands of floss, embroider the stems with two rows of stem stitch, referring to page 9. Appliqué bowl pieces A and C to the background. Remove any markings and press.

2. Add the print border, referring to page 60.

3. Baste for quilting, referring to page 60. Quilt using the inner stitching line of the pear pattern on page 52 in a random and overlapping style. Quilt through the border to the edge. Quilt behind the remaining bowl piece B to keep the quilt flat. Remove any markings and basting.

4. Add binding to the quilt, referring to page 61.

5. From the patterns on pages 51–52, trace and cut two bowl pieces B, two pears, two bananas, and two apples. For bowl, pear, apple, and banana, sew the pieces with right sides together and on top of a piece of cotton batting. Sew around using a ¼" seam and leave an opening for turning. Trim the batting close to the seamline and clip seam allowances as needed. Turn right side out and press. I quilted the bowl with large random clamshells.

6. Appliqué the fruit in place, referring to the photograph for placement. Add the bowl piece B. Appliqué around except for the two spaces as noted on the pattern at the top of the bowl. Use a few extra stitches at all dots to secure.

7. Using a leaf pattern on page 59, make 4 leaves referring to page 12. Using the 2" circles, make four bead fruit for cherries, referring to page 17. Add one leaf to the bunch. Using the 1¾" circles and 10mm beads, make seven berries, referring to page 16. Add three leaves to form a berry cluster. Slide the cherries and berries into the open slots on the bowl top. Bend the wires to arrange the fruit.

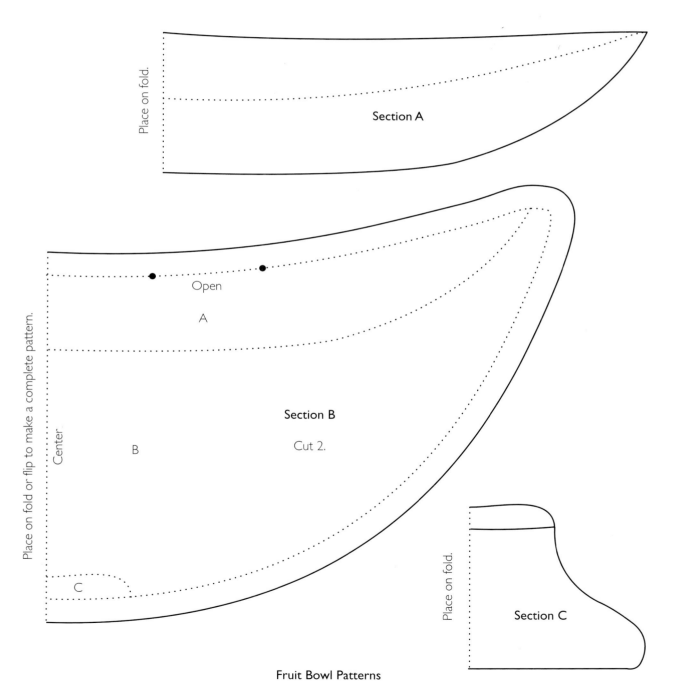

Place on fold.

Section A

Place on fold or flip to make a complete pattern.

Open

A

Center

B

Section B

Cut 2.

C

Place on fold.

Section C

Fruit Bowl Patterns

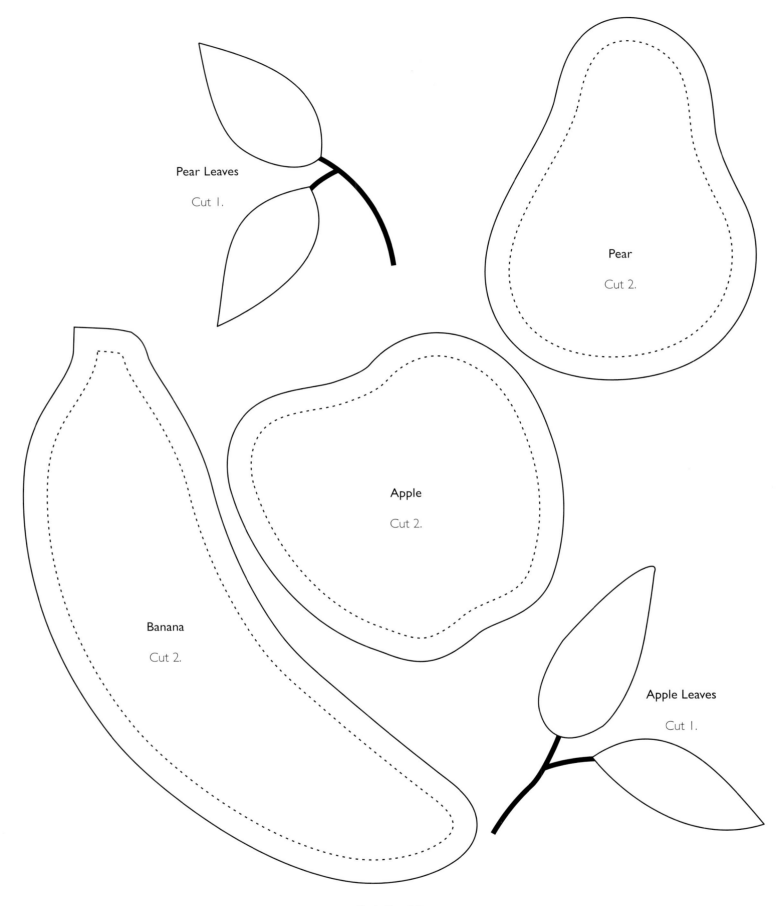

Pear Leaves

Cut 1.

Pear

Cut 2.

Apple

Cut 2.

Banana

Cut 2.

Apple Leaves

Cut 1.

Fruit Bowl Patterns

Flower Vases

Finished size: 13½" x 17½"

Fill any of these three vase shapes with a bouquet of
stemmed flowers. The quilts are extra easy to make.
The magic comes when you add the flowers, berries, and leaves.
What a great way to give a gift of flowers that never fade!

Materials and Cutting

Fabric requirements are based on approximately 42"-wide cotton fabric.

For each quilt you will need:

Fabric	Cutting
⅔ **yard muslin** for background and backing	One 8½" x 12½" piece for background; one 16" x 20" piece for backing
¼ **yard print** for border	Two 3"-wide strips
Small pieces assorted fabrics for flowers, leaves, and vase	See Step 7 on page 55 for the flowers I used.
¼ **yard binding**	Two 2"-wide strips
Cotton batting for vase	6" x 7"
Batting	16" x 20"

Other Materials:
- wire, beads, floral tape, glue (optional)
- threads to match vase fabric and yo-yo fabrics
- natural-color quilting thread

Assembly

1. Sew the border to the background, referring to page 60.

2. Referring to the patterns on pages 55–56, trace and cut two of the vase that you select. Sew the vase pieces with right sides together on top of a batting piece, using a ¼" seam. Leave an opening at the bottom for turning. Trim the batting close to the seamline and clip seam allowances as needed. Turn right side out and press.

3. Baste for quilting, referring to page 60. Quilt through the borders to the edge, using these tips for each version:

> **Lavender**—Sketch a six-pointed star at the top half of the quilt. Echo quilt outward from the points to the outer edge of the border. Fill in the interior with random clamshells. For the vase, quilt basic diagonal lines crossing in the center.

Lavender

Christmas—Quilt a large feather in the background area. Radiate lines in a sunburst pattern from the center of the quilt outward. For the vase, quilt large random clamshells from the top downward.

Autumn (shown on page 53)—Break the area into sections using double curving lines. Fill these spaces with randomly marked cross-hatching. For the vase, quilt the bottom with random clamshells about two-thirds of the way up. Finish the top with cross-hatching.

4. Remove any markings and basting.

5. Add binding to the quilt, referring to page 61.

6. Appliqué the vase in place leaving most of the top open. Tack down the center of the tops of the vases with wider mouths.

7. Add flowers of your choice, using long stems on each. For the Autumn Basket, I made one five-petal posie on page 15, two saucer flowers on page 14, and two bead roses on page 16. For the Lavender Vase, I made three poppies on page 14, five florets on page 14, and two buds on page 18. For the Christmas Vase, I made three roses on page 17 and six berries on page 16.

Christmas

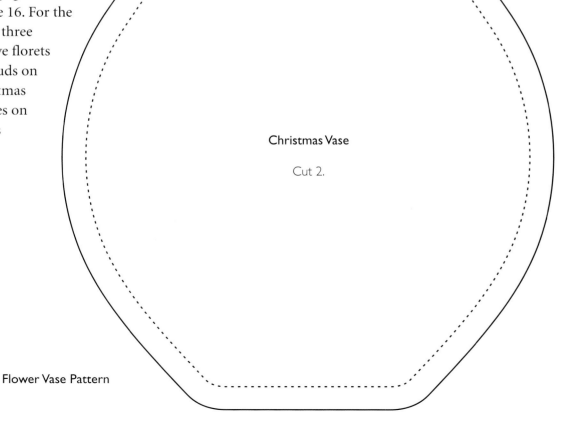

Christmas Vase

Cut 2.

Flower Vase Pattern

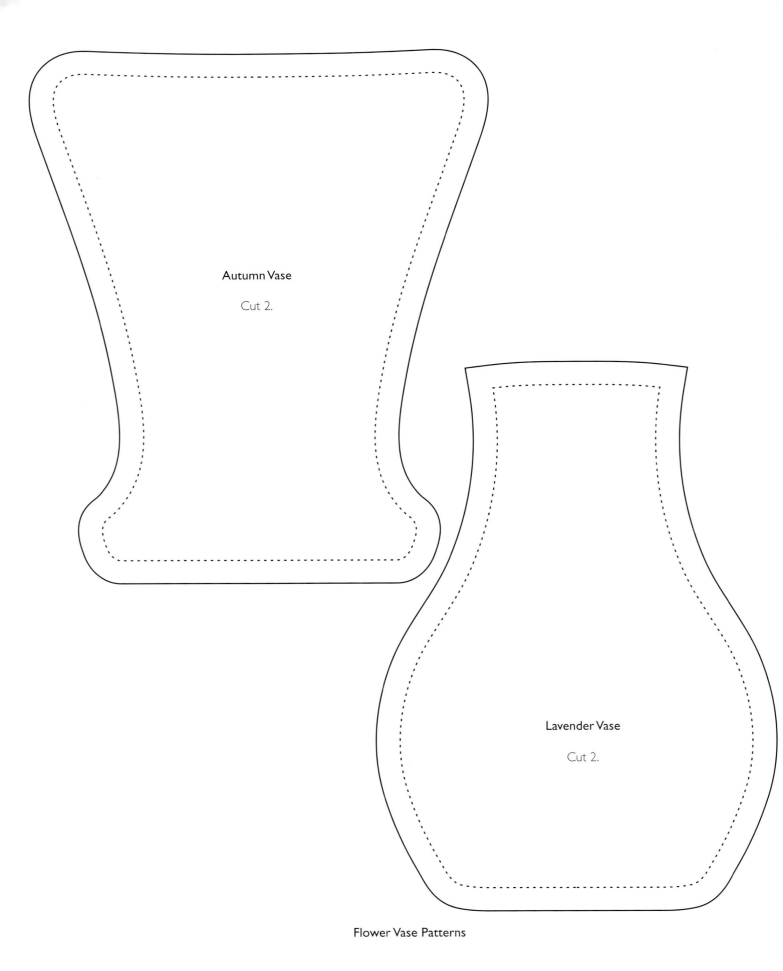

Autumn Vase

Cut 2.

Lavender Vase

Cut 2.

Flower Vase Patterns

More Projects

These gathered flowers, leaves, and berries are great for creating quick and easy craft projects that call for bright and beautiful blooms. Try these fun ideas or create your own. Remember, you can mix and match the flowers in the projects to get just the look you want.

Gift Boxes

Slide a few posies into the bow of a wrapped and ribboned box to add a special touch to any gift.

Sachet

Catch a few blooms in the bow of a simple fabric sachet bag. Fold a 10" x 9" piece of fabric in half and sew the side and bottom seams. Add lace at the top edge and fill with potpourri. Tie it closed with a decorative ribbon and tuck in a few fabric flowers.

Tussie Mussie

Combine your favorite fabric blooms into a small bouquet wrapped together with floral tape. Nestle the bouquet into a circle of gathered lace. Use a 12" or longer piece of 4" or wider lace. Secure in place with stitches or glue.

Napkin Ring

Cover a 1"-wide cardboard ring with fabric using thick white glue. I cut my ring from a paper towel core, or you could use a purchased napkin ring. Wrap the stem of any flower with a leaf around the ring using the blossom to hide the stem wraps. Perfect for a garden tea.

Containers

A basket, a vase, or a small watering can make great flower containers. I stuffed some natural excelsior into the basket and watering can. This will hold any combination of flowers and leaves in place. What a great idea for party favors!

Jewelry

Combine the fabric "bead" with glass beads to make a stunning necklace. The glass beads add the weight missing in the fabric ones. Your local fabric and bead shops will provide endless combinations. I love the idea of making jewelry from our much-loved fabric stashes.

Patterns

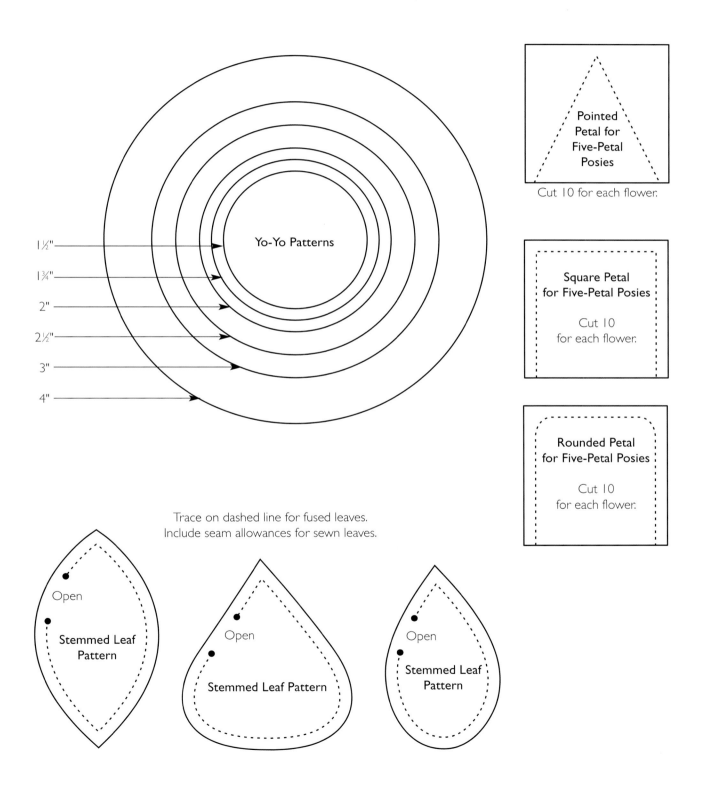

Yo-Yo Patterns

1½"
1¾"
2"
2½"
3"
4"

Pointed Petal for Five-Petal Posies

Cut 10 for each flower.

Square Petal for Five-Petal Posies

Cut 10 for each flower.

Rounded Petal for Five-Petal Posies

Cut 10 for each flower.

Trace on dashed line for fused leaves.
Include seam allowances for sewn leaves.

Open
Stemmed Leaf Pattern

Open
Stemmed Leaf Pattern

Open
Stemmed Leaf Pattern

Quilting Basics

Borders

Borders complement the simple floral designs of the quilts. They are like a mat and frame for a picture. Most of the borders are added after the quilt has been appliquéd, embroidered, and trimmed to size.

Begin by measuring the sides of the appliquéd center and cut the side borders to that length.

Using a ¼" seam allowance, sew the side borders to the quilt and press toward the border. Then measure the top and bottom, including the side borders, and cut the borders to that measurement. Repeat to add a second border.

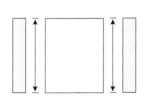
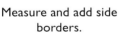

Measure and add side borders.

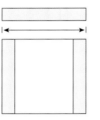

Measure and add top and bottom borders.

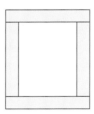

Completed border.

Quilting

I prefer to hand quilt and mark quilting lines only when necessary because I like to add the quilting as I go without drawing lines. For those of you who prefer marking, use a blue removable marker or a white fabric pencil for dark fabrics. Mark lightly, but make sure you can easily see your lines and remember to remove them before pressing.

Properly preparing the layers for hand quilting will ensure a nice flat quilt. I quilt without a frame or hoop, which works well for smaller quilts. Cut the batting and backing at least an inch larger than the quilt top all around. Lay out the backing wrong side up. Place the batting on top and add the quilt top right side up. Baste the layers together with long stitches using white thread. Baste in a grid with lines from side to side in both directions and about 4" apart. This will keep your layers secure as you quilt.

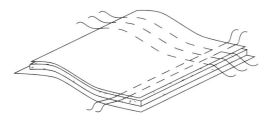

I use a simple running stitch that goes through all three layers of fabric. Use an 18"-long piece of quilting thread. Tie a knot and pull it between the layers (inside the batting) to begin quilting.

To end a thread, make a knot close to the quilt top and pull it into the batting. Let the needle travel between the layers for an inch or so then come up and snip. I generally quilt from the center outward or from one end or side to the other.

What to quilt? Designs are endless. Create a shape, radiate lines, use traditional feathers or cross-hatching, or stitch the elegant simplicity of echoing lines. I quilt one area first and then decide what to do next rather than planning the entire design beforehand. Sketch possibilities on paper to use as reference when creating patterns. Combining multiple patterns can produce fantastic results. Just let loose and stitch.

Binding

After the piece is quilted and the basting is removed, trim the batting and backing even with the outer edge of the outer border unless otherwise indicated. I use a single fold binding, stitching it on with a ½" seam allowance.

Cut the strips 2" wide from selvage to selvage using a rotary cutter, ruler, and mat. Stitch

the binding first on the sides then the top and bottom of the quilt.

Turn the binding to the back and fold the raw edge under about ½". Fold the binding once more and blindstitch it down being careful not to let any stitches go through to the front.

Adding Bindings

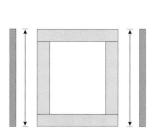

Measure and add side bindings.

Measure and add top and bottom bindings.

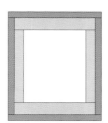

Binding ready to turn back

To make the corner folds on the back, miter the corners following the illustrations. I pin the entire binding in place before stitching it down on the back. Once your binding is done, always sign and date your finished quilt.

Stitch side binding to the quilt. Press binding out.

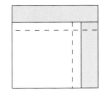

Stitch top binding to the quilt. Press binding out.

Fold top strip.

Fold again.

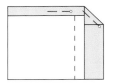

Fold side strip at 45° angle.

Fold as shown.

Fold again.

Quilt front